STARTING *from* ANYWHERE
LEX RUNCIMAN

salmonpoetry

Published in 2009 by
Salmon Poetry
Cliffs of Moher, County Clare, Ireland
Website: www.salmonpoetry.com
Email: info@salmonpoetry.com

ISBN 978-1-907056-10-9

Cover photography: Lex Runciman
Cover design & typesetting: Siobhán Hutson

for my parents

Acknowledgements

Grateful acknowledgement is made to the editors of the following publications where these works or earlier versions of them first appeared:

Poetry East: One Thing My Mother Always Said
South Dakota Review: "All Is a Procession" and "I Wonder If Everything Has a Soul?"
Salt River Review: "Joy Cometh in the Morning"
Valparaiso Poetry Review: Broadmoor, How Dawn Begins and "I Noticed the Peaches"
Ekphrasis: "Hammer and Sickle, 1928" and "Young Woman Standing at a Virginal"
basalt: Lear in Bed, At Castlerigg, Cumbria, and "Time Lies All Around Us"
Fine Madness: "Nothing Happened That Night" and "Immediately After Christmas, the Mood Lightened in Manor Road"
Rock & Sling: A Good Day and "It's As Beckoning as Heaven"
Caffeine Destiny: Beginning
Water-Stone Review: Postcard from the Tate: 'My Parents,' by David Hockney
Hubbub: In My Alternate Life
Windfall: Pacific or Not
Fireweed: Night Sky Northwest
Oregon Humanities: When Fictions Are Facts
Free Verse (Wisconsin): "What Was There Before and Is There Still"
The Linfield Review: Oak Fallen
Rivendell: Another Rose Festival Parade

"A Greeting of Books" was commissioned by President Vivian Bull to help commemorate the inauguration of The Jerold Nicholson Library at Linfield College.

Love and thanks to my many teachers, to my good and generous colleagues at Linfield College, to Chris Anderson and Lee Bassett, to Jessie Lendennie and Siobhán Hutson, to Lisa Steinman and Eric Muller, and to Beth and Jane, and Debbie, every day.

Contents

1

In My Alternate Life

In my alternate life
I visit *Untitled, 1949* every Sunday afternoon,
        and sometimes it hangs in a kitchen
and sometimes in a tea room in Abergavenney in Wales.
    In my alternate life I'm Chinese or Brazilian.
I'm walking a beach scattered with slate, it being Cornwall.
    Hills, hedgerows, stoats, and a prairie of flowers,
and my mother sleeps in a hammock
        and my father sketches her into a book.
    I order at the lunch counter
that was Nighthawks the night before.
    I sit on the stool opposite the coffee urns.
My old back feels sturdy as it did when I was eight,
    sun lights the ochre wall like terracotta jazz,
nobody bothers me, the cup never drained.
How have I forgotten the name of this piazza,
        Florence, the one with Dante
swirling his stone cloak? Walk three blocks any way
and I'll be lost.
    Sometimes swans, sometimes vultures.
Air sings oxygen like after lightning.
    Boredom slides like a dime under a cushion.
It perches like a pigeon on my head.
        And if I want to talk with someone,
there he is – young or old, American or dead or not –
    there she is. Stars anytime.
Imagination scares me less.
People are tolerant and the world is just.

Birds

If you go to Down House, the leather boots
 under the bench by the back door
could not belong to Charles Darwin.
But the birds (beaks hard, feathers faded),
the birds in the glass case in the first floor hall –

if you were a better ornithologist you might
 imagine their time and places,
how they were etherized,
singly, reverently, in a glass jar, then gutted
 with a small blade, stuffed
and arranged for beauty and for study.

Famous above the iguanas, they perch on
 stick bushes and no longer startle
any of Emma's children, lamp in hand, sleepless
 at 3 a.m. –
not William, Etty, George, Bessy, Francis, Leonard,
 Horace, or Annie,

Annie, who died in 1851 at the age of ten,
who asked her father once if they had names.
"Only finches," he said.
 "No, they should have names."
A fair, fresh day. So he took her hand
and led her outside
 for a walk.

"Foxglove, Bedstraw, Meadowsweet, Cow Parsley, Ragged Robin"

– Gillian Clark

Woke to watery sun
and this morning the first
we've had day and weather for such a walk
        over low wet hills –
    to range and roam where oxen tilled
and tired arms scythed a thousand years
and find in that hour ample for our harvesting
       purple-thimbled foxglove
and bedstraw, meadowsweet, cow parsley, ragged
         robin, their tips ripe not with tears
but a night's own sweet work.

They exhale
      and they weight the arm. The sun ascends
and warms as over pasture and by soft hedgerows
we loop and arrive at our start, laden
      and made quiet,
sated and happy to trim and to arrange
in the water of a wide mouth bell of glass
      stems and colour we had no hand in making,
and for itself praise each,
and all their bright refusal to be kept.

Self Portrait

Understanding the transience of
    time and place and what happens
to every fleshly body, he has
anticipated this occasion: he sat down
    one afternoon, took a seat at
a table by a window, arranged his paper and
began by mirror to make himself, forehead
creased, wide-set eyes, broad nose,
    moustache, cleft chin, jowly
in a frock coat, a hat
wider, taller than a bowler,
    window lace over his right shoulder,
a gentle breeze
fluttering with his name inscribed:
    Rembrandt 1648.

All else dense by lines, light
    is the untouched: glass and sky,
a sheaf of drawings in a stack,
a loose cuff, his right thumb and fingers
    poised as he holds the stylus.
Your looking and his collide.
    His face makes plain that
now, having asked his largest question,
he will wait for as long as you think,
    as long as you choose.
And what you answer he will draw.

Convergences

1.

Warm in full sun, we use the largest boulders as seats,
unlace our shoes, pull off our socks, swerve and dawdle
into wind, and someone must watch the waves ashore.

Gulls caw. Pelicans love a line along a swell.
You notice, watching the waves ashore, how singular
each wave is. You notice, watching the waves ashore,

some pools blue deeper than knees. Sanderlings hurry.
Cormorants dive. And someone, someone, someone,
someone − someone must watch the waves ashore.

2.

Birds call and call. A low eastern sun rises warm.
Wind eases among palms, over the floral hedge,
drifts over the steady gather and small roar −

the shore break, salt water neither cool nor warm,
vague green as it fluffs and swirls coarse sand
that goes deeper underfoot until you swim

awkward, as land muscles unknot and lengthen
into a rhythm, inhale and heartbeat, one sea
inside, the other filling your ears.

Each swell lifts you a foot or so, the beach from here
a postcard: sand and palms. Hang onto this −
qualities of air, how, resting, buoyant, you look up:

on water whirling through all the empyrean
you are floated by the earth.

Little Girl, Lost Cap

Inside the café inside the bookstore
on Wednesday before Thanksgiving
a family sat at a wide table. One of them,
short but a veteran walker, approached us.
She touched the red fabric eyelevel
and featuring a pattern of pears, apples,
red and blue grapes. "What's this?"
"It's a table cloth." "Who put it here?"
"It was here when we sat down."
She looked at the fruit. "Oh."
Half an hour later that family has gone,
and the hat on the floor must have belonged
to that girl. It's cream coloured wool
with a circle of loops of deep navy,
then an inch of blue. Hand knit.
Yesterday it was pulled over a small girl's
black, curly hair as she ran from a car
to catch up to her sisters and brother
opening a back door.
Now it's lost — it's here.
What happens never happens again.

1972

The chaplain sat at his desk. Have we met?
No. But you want me to support your conscientious
Objection — you want me to write a letter. *Yes.*
Let me ask some questions. Could you kill someone —
An intruder to save yourself? *No.* What about
To save your mother or wife from rape? *Yes.*
Save a sister or daughter? *Yes.*

Where are you from? *Oregon.*
Do you love your country? *Yes.*
Would you serve the United States? *Yes.*
Would you kill its sworn enemies? *No.*
You would kill an intruder to save your family? *Yes.*
But not an enemy of the United States? *No.*

Methodist, Lutheran, Catholic, Quaker —
Do you practice any religion? *No.*
Believe in God? *I don't understand the question.*
You're afraid. *Yes.* You're afraid of battle. *Yes.*
Of letting others down? *Yes.* And these
Are your conscientious objections? *Yes, no.*
When ordered by a superior officer, would you kill?
I don't know, no, I would have to decide.
Wouldn't it be too late for that? *Yes,*
It would be too late.

You're a coward: you're a coward
And you want me to help get you off the hook.
I looked at him. Are you afraid? *Yes.*
You say you love your country? *Yes.*
You could kill to save your family? *Yes, yes.*
Then why are you here — what are you afraid of?
Loyalties and confusions, I should have said.
Infinities, the worth of a day.

A Good Day

I'm wary of belief, but not emphatically.
The look ground squirrels give the sky
focuses an intensity that seems instructional:
here's how to stand upright if you must.

Though generally I like them, I'm wary of
people who must tell me their sex lives and
    charities.
Their motives confuse me and friendship is
confusing enough.

Despite the indifference of high clouds, the
    flooded green
May gives towards the solstice, despite the ways
clothes hang and rugs recline, not once saying
    thank-you or even no,
humming along is fine with me.

I seek air clean, water clear, ecologies galore.
I wish it were easier.

Talk to interesting people, and a day both dilates
    and constricts: it's late, where did the time go?
They've been places I haven't, and most of them
    haven't killed anyone.
A few have. Others are less sure.
I think about orders and who gives them.
I think about laws.

I don't know if this is true – that I won't claim
    anything if it means violence wins.
I don't want to make it a contest, not even checkers.
If lucky, you can do this, maybe not every day
    but many.
Today, so far so good.

"In Step and On Time"

— Charles Wright

In step and on time — *there*'s a wish.
The child was a neighbour, unspeaking
and deaf. She visited sometimes
when even two doors down we could hear
angry voices, her parents' pans hitting walls.
She would knock, neither too loudly nor softly,

and eventually we kept for her crayons
and paper she'd colour just for colour.
Later yet she learned she could put her own
graham crackers on a plate, and pour a glass of milk.
She asked of us so little, but her parents
fought often and sometimes at inconvenient hours.

Once when I was hurried, when she could not stay,
she spilled it all — crackers soggy,
milk white over the table and onto the floor.
I picked her up, she was six,
and set her down outside, and shut the door.
I never saw her face. Then later I felt terrible.

The afternoon she came back,
she carried in one hand a plate of crackers
and in the other a full glass of milk.

"Joy Cometh in the Morning"

Psalm 30

Brakes fail. We lie.
Carrots stick in the gullet,
   coughing triggers a stroke.
Rain freezes. A runner on stairs
   unmoors itself and slides.
Against all justice, the baby sickens.
   A woman putting on the thirteenth green
dizzies, her last words, "my head aches,"
   and "take me home."
War hovers. Your watch is off.
   What child deserves such parents?
Dead fish clog the river, wash ashore,
   then the smell begins. Someone's son
strangles a person he thinks he loves.
   Crops wilt. The knife slips.
Ridicule leads to bruises.
   That person listens and walks away,
and that one, who said the wrong things,
   knows it. No touch endures.
The doctor is unsure.
   Memory says love is unreturned.
The words you have rehearsed
   vanish from your mouth. Sleep
teases. Gesture is not enough.
   I don't know how we go on.

One Thing My Mother Always Said

"You'd lose your head if it wasn't attached."
And I do lose things – pens, notes, books.
I can picture the brown spine, gold lettering,
    The Poems of William Butler Yeats,
And see the shelf, the gap where Yeats was
    and isn't. I can see the 1960 yellow Chevy
In the driveway we no longer own.
I see a photo of my children on a beach.
They're playing in the dunes – hide and seek.
    Over here … Over here.

"Taking Any Route, Starting from Anywhere"
– T.S. Eliot

Old contemplations, earth and heaven, the small
    nave's ancient chevrons smooth:
Little Gidding, Huntingdonshire – flat country
unlike Wales, the Lake District's tarns and fells.
You're welcomed, welcome to toll the bell.
They have the date he signed the visitor's book;
    they have the book.

Pond water glazed, bushes delicate with hoarfrost
    in mid-winter spring,
or vivid in green spring or dulled in summer leaf –
whatever the route, however you arrive, place
    merely conspires:
mountainside, city bridge, parking lot, beach,
    or lawn dropped with dew.
It would be this way once only: origins without
    metaphor, there and then, here and now.

Eliot saw Little Gidding once, May time, 1936.
We arrived in January wet and afternoon dark,
and sat blank in the damp and unlit chapel where
    prayer was valid.
Then outside, roaming that yard, we found a
child's grave, and it stopped us.
Moon and sun, it stopped us – so recently made
    earth's own dirt said no name.

At the Wolf Creek Inn

The effort always to be *here* — a veranda,
second floor at the Wolf Creek Inn, circa 1883,
summer green apples plumping in a canopy
opposite a thirsty birch.

Mary Pickford, Jack London, Clark Gable,
Orson Wells — all slept here. Four miles upriver,
all that remains of Golden drifts and ghosts
in a dream neither church nor placer mines confirmed.

From this valley's sides, leafy, red-trunk madrona
loop and angle stoic for rain, easy
and deep in their non-advocacy. Nothing I see calls me
to cut it down, dynamite it or sluice it through screens.

Dark rises. The day's last slow light
goes an ashy rose, a breeze
over trout asleep in Coyote Canyon Creek.
Hawks never ask to whom the earth belongs.

"All Is a Procession"

— Walt Whitman

The oaks out my window,
the roads and byways of their great bark
sometimes exposed, sometimes by mosses thickened,
moss green all seasons but August, the green then
almost rust —

the oaks out my window, columns wide at the ground
and thinning higher, splitting, branching and splitting,
rivers draining air into the sea of the ground
and the ground's water rising to every smaller streams
and dissipations, each leaf all that rustles
quiet in the currents of day, noisy
in the currents of the dark —
my arms cannot circle the oaks out my window.

Their age not of grandfathers or mothers
but grand dozen mothers and fathers
who idled under those winter-bare scaffolds
and marked their own breath as they looked up at snow,
who dozed in June's warm and insect whine,
stared at shadow and shadow and thought of
what next to do
and stood then and walked away —
the oaks out my window balk account.

Mistletoe thick in their crowns balks account,
and lichen sleeving their slender arms,
flags of ferns
aloft in their branched hollows,
birds fond of acorns and squirrels fond of acorns,
worms inside puff-balls like decorations hung —
all balk account.

All evolution, iris and lens, aqueous humours,
                    heart and bronchial trees,
and tympanum, hammer, stirrup and anvil,
the meanders of finger pads each itself,
and jays territorial, and quail, song swallows,
the voice that calls and the voice that answers –
by accidents, by causes and endless effects
all evolution has led alike
to the oaks out my window.

I see them every day and they balk account
as does my happiness seeing them.

"We're Drowning in Explanations"
— Shirley Hazzard

Wheels, gears, handlebars, washers, nuts,
    two pedals, one seat, three tools — the bicycle
in all its parts bulges
a corrugated box soaked in transit, instructions
    blurred to gray.

And thus does the world's surface carry
    its names — unconsciously,
with no knowledge of their uses.
Same for animals, trees, plants, mosses, lichen.
Yet it's hard to do this, to get around the names.
You have to look quick and think not at all.

In the morning, when I half wake and air and a
    dim light seem more hospitable
than any before or after, sometimes
I'm looking at another person who's not a
    person to me then so much as skin visible or
a sound that resolves to breathing but which, then,
    is just *whoosh*, just air motion.

To wake like this is comfortable and unspeakable
    in the moment: it is to not know, to not remember
you're not knowing. It is
merely to inhabit sensation happily.

"The Heart Wants What It Wants"

– Emily Dickinson

Seeing – a little Distraction –
A harrier aloft
Chased by white feathers

Under that tree
A summer afternoon dozes Eternity –
And red-shouldered birds hector crows

What the heart wants – winter's early dark
Settled as wool – August thunder
stampeding the cattle –

Calm in doubt –
Love it has no reason – but Wish –
to expect –

In Snow Fog

Cedars lust for definition.
And red alders, their fractal crowns
       gauzy, they retreat
and never advance near enough.
Over and over wherever they are
they disappear
and the stars decline.

* * *

Moon's eye,
       the laughters of water.

Or beauty unnecessary.
The genocidal dead unwilling to comprehend,
       unable to go home. Or music
before it finds the harmonies,
       the drift and lilt of notes –

on the right day, the correct afternoon
       after which it will be gone,
you walk in it and through it and not quite entirely
out – place and presence, a monochrome
taking its own time
       saying what it has to say.

* * *

Where, when we are done with them
and they with us, where do our sins go –
       not the polite untruths to make a kindness,
not even the lack of attention selfishness makes.
       I mean what anger does
for its own terror that will not be satisfied.
Willed violence, the conscious choice.

★ ★ ★

If, as Emerson believed, earth and its humours
make the one book of God we might read
      being here, being qualified,
then what is snow fog but notes in the margin,
a hieroglyph, one cuneiform again and again?
Collective, associate, it loiters after a night of thaw,
      after a day of gravity and exhale,
after two nights and a day utterly blind cold,
      unlined and de-horizoned
to become at last snow's fluff and dust
      that will not settle and will not rise.

2

"To Own What Is Lost"

— Lee Bassett

After cola, three corn dogs, a froth of cotton candy,
you can imagine what he looked for.
   "OK?" He nodded.
His state celebrates its 100th birthday,
and what he will remember is sick first, then
     so much better he's thirsty.

Later the boy and his Grandpa
walk into one of those high saggy tents,
climb paint-flakey bleachers and sit and look up.
He sees people wearing swimsuits
     step off small platforms. They kick
and swing, do not fall, and one of them lets go
     and then gets caught –
lets go, somersaults, and then gets caught.

He has never seen this before. He knows
his sins killed Jesus –
     whoever Jesus was, whatever sins are.
He looks up, watches hard and cannot and dare not
stop. He believes that if he fails, if he
     blinks or rubs his eyes or sneezes or looks away,
one or the other of these will fall
with no branch to catch them.

The man and woman swing, cross, rise
wider and higher than any platform. How
     can he see them at the same time? Then
a new slender woman dips her hands into a pan, claps
a white cloud, grabs a bar,
     coils herself and swings. Then
on the other side
another man
     muscled hairy-chested and wide-shouldered
salutes the crowd and toes the edge and jumps.

Postcard from the Tate: "My Parents," by David Hockney

A table between them, they sit on slat chairs.
Mother's hands hold each other in her lap.
Wearing a high-necked, long-sleeved dress,
    blue, with brown shoes – slippers or loafers –
she gazes from that deep repose
lack of conversation makes: she's bored but
    used to waiting – she wants to be supportive.

Half-blind, too proud for glasses,
Father hunches and peers at his paper.
The heels of his black oxfords lift off the ground –
    he's that tense. He reads with the concentration
Churchill brought to war,
because he hates just sitting while someone
    paints or takes a picture.
He hates tulips on the table, the vase, all display –
he has agreed to this only because his son's success
    is discussed now in the *Times*.

The mystery, like God, is David Hockney –
everything in the square summoned by him,
arranged and made persistent by his art.
Yet these are also merely his parents
    who long ago rose from those folding chairs.
Never having met them, never having seen
    the painting, only its postcard,
how is it possible then, this genuine affection?

"Their Smiles at the Camera
Are of Genuine Delight"

— Ian McEwan

Warmth on their shoulders, a mild expression
of May wind lifting their hair —

how far from death my only parents have come.
Trees blur behind them.

Behind the trees, behind their eyes,
live all their days and months to that *now*.

They see Big Lake blue with sky, a noisy creek,
dragonflies, water striders in the shallows.

Their happiness is intimate, one body known and
near to one body known and near,

and a basket
with sandwiches, apples, brie and beer.

Broadmoor

That July day the near smoke rose,
we walked 78th past Cedar and Laurel
and watched the Whittlesey house burn.

One year snow fell taller that I was,
burying every bush: a squeaky white,
a cold, unfillable quiet.

Hills there rolled on one another.
The ambulance saved the woman bleeding.
Once snagged, the kite never came down.

Leaves overhead, leaves underfoot,
and milk quartz watery in the creek.
What oiled-rock road

ever met a knee it couldn't love?
Run fast enough, a hive
can be thrown like a football.
Place is time.

"I Wonder If Everything Has a Soul?"

– Ellen Glasgow

By which Dorinda meant not planks, pails, hand trucks,
the store and station at Peddlar's Mill – she meant
broomsedge, Virginia's scrub at dusk in winter, the train
leaving a snowy silence, fields tired as the faces of horses.

On the ridge where I lived as a child, old roads
meandered contours under firs. I learned distance,
rise and fall by bicycle. I thought the trees I climbed
had souls. One, a big leaf maple, had so arranged itself

branches made a ladder, then a split seat –
trunk for a back, thirty feet invisible and aloft.
I liked a breeze easy in those leaves. Stronger wind
only made a roar, a slightly dizzy, swaying grace.

At the right time of year up there, I'd let go seeds
and count the seconds they spun.
I knew then souls lived in any live shape –
maple souls, cat souls, wiener dog souls.
I was pretty sure.

"The Truth Is Never Loud"

— Marjorie Sandor

The noise became hearable only after her
    death, which was sudden.
No one played the radio, no one hummed.
When we emptied the house, rooms
    echoed, and ghosts with their cigarettes
    and freshened cocktails
sat down at card tables.
The women wore rouge and pearls, the men
    wingtips and diamond tacked ties.
Someone shuffled. Others sipped
    vodka martinis or Early Times mist.
They chatted about work, children, husbands,
    wives — who crashed a car,
was pulled over drunk, fell from a roof, or
    cheated, or heard from the docs bad news.
They picked up their cards,
the room quiet as they sorted aces, faces
and numbers into suits, and totalled
    the count to answer or bid, these being,
as they understood them, peaceful hours,
rain outside, late Friday into Saturday,
    drinks freshened and time yet — no hurry.

"Time Lies All Around Us"

— Peter Davison

Under the bed, the sweaters of 1954 surrender,
    all that Korean armistice joy fraying,
Buddy Holly's "Flower of My Heart"
    leaking from an elbow, Doris Day's soprano,
a red-topped Nash slick and well in Detroit.
The horse hair Chesterfield remembers
    sweet noons in deep clover, Jim Crow cotton
dyed and tight-stretched for the brass tack line,
    mustard gas, radio tubes, Rilke meeting Freud,
my grandmother in her thick brogue
rebuking a pastor whose name is lost.
    A phone rings in my pocket.
Why do I think of half a robin's egg, emptied,
    a scrim of yellow — a bowl in the grass.
I picked it up. Cracks I'd not seen widened
to nothing I could fix. I took it to my mother,
    who looked, and to my father, who nodded.
I once held quiet in the cup of my skin —
weightless space, failure, o that blue.

"Nothing Happened That Night"

– Kurt Vonnegut

Hot dark, humid dark.
Half moon peach red, summer fires
haze in the eyes and pepper in the throat.
Only half the dipper's there,
and I don't know what rises
innocent as this beat and saw–whine of bugs.

I knew someone who smoked like this –
unfiltered Chesterfield after Chesterfield,
a rhythm of his own disgust.
That was after he quit the vodka.
None of it worked, none of it brought her back.
Even before, I didn't think he loved her –

I'm still not sure.
I don't forgive my failures.
What he did nights like this
drunk for years, then sober,
was sit out in the dark, not answer
and not come in.

Lear in Bed

Once he slept in a basket of laundry
and woke when she scolded him his mudded shoes.

Once in an estuary he swam with seals, their black coats.
Now only cold arrives, the window iced thick as his wrist.

He is turned and washed as an infant, hands on the covers
arranged. He is not privy to helplessness that would be insult

if he knew it. His brother, who died pruning a tree,
has arrived still gloved, still sweaty from that trouble.

When the fog clears, he will pace the rolling ground
of a wheat field, estimating a price at bushels per acre.

Sun in his eyes, this would be a good place to stop.

Another Rose Festival Parade

Once two dead men carried a ladder between them
four blocks to a corner where they set it up,
wood stairs to nowhere, looked to the sky
for comment on likely weather, then lit cigarettes
which killed them, but not that day.

It seemed odd to me – a ladder among blankets
and chairs, all kinds of people sitting on the curb
or wandering, buying ice cream or talking to the police.
Then the first car came, the first horse and rider,
and I got it: we climbed the rungs – me,
my father, then his, and there we stood
as all moved past. Taller than anyone,
I was hungry and had to pee.

What we spoke of on that ladder
I do not remember. What they honoured
taking me there, I did not fathom. Mostly,
they scared me – love and fear.
I lost my sweater.
Sun burned my arms to peeling.
But I still like marching bands –
percussion and brass, rhythm and tune –
the one in the distance, the one playing now.

How Dawn Begins

Turkeys feeding lift their wattled heads to look.
Deer with mange browse Meeker's woods,
and in Ecuador a high, white-seared geography of cloud
slides over a hill of coffee flowering.

My mother's words, the soft under her eyes,
her shoes, her kettle steaming, radio on,
all come back to me if I think hard,
wait, not yet, listen, ok, now.

No Store, No Car

The West Slope Piggly Wiggly grocery store is
    immaterial now, purely memory, but
inside its swung door, shiny steel carts nest.
Pull one out, the bottom clanks down,
a grid of space opens for bananas, milk in bottles,
    peanuts scooped into a squared paper bag.
A quick stop, so I'm waiting in the car,
    a 1950 Chevy sedan, sun yellow, white-walls,
three speeds on the column, a hump down the middle
    and Saint Christopher on the dash.
The engine ticks and cools. Seats go door to door.
Only one wing window cranks open.
This knob pulls out, pushes halfway, then in.
    This one turns and clicks.
This one moves a red line over numbers.
    That lipstick is my mother's.
That button pushes but it doesn't start anything.
You have to look both ways. You have to
slide your hands over the bumps because
    the wheel won't turn.
You have to kneel, you have to be the engine.
When you see her, grin, honk the horn, wave.

Goodbye is Hello

Smoked to the thumb, red inhale and ghost,
an unfiltered Chesterfield sparks over stars
    and hisses into the watered lawn.
Work tired, he surveys for the evening's last
    time: gerbera daisies, bridal spirea, impatiens,
    rhododendron, the fecund of flowers.
He liked vodka and Angostura bitters.
Vermouth, rum, bourbon, all the siblings and
    cousins, romance of olives, wit and repartee,
the blank oblivious of America and of success.
Our dead depart, but they stay.
They haunt the dahlias, the crocus and rose and
    snowdrop.
Rhododendron mouth their words.

I think after death they rub their eyes.
They study us not to admonish nor apologise or
    give advice,
but to guess at what little of their breathing on earth
    survives their ecstasies and angers,
their boredom and their going away.
What one says may be smart as a pig snout, wet
    as slick fish.
What one says is true is wobbly as bull's eye
    glass, the self's mirror, sponge and rock.

What one says stays and vanishes and overlays.
Gestures and all their confusions ring like rain.
And kale and the four lips of the dogwood
    answer in their season.

When Fictions Are Facts

A dozen or so miles south of McMinnville on highway 99, the Bethel-Lincoln road offers drivers a back way into Salem. The pavement runs straight through grass fields before it makes a series of sweeping turns, including one that skirts a hillside pioneer cemetery.

Whenever I've reached that corner, I've thought of stopping to wander among the headstones, their names less familiar now – Eustace, Ephraim, Walter, Maude. And though they would all be strangers to me, at least some of them must have descendants alive today, descendants able to match lived history with the names and dates. I have no such names in my past, because I have no knowledge of my parents or grandparents or where they came from or where they are buried.

What I know of my past starts with what my parents told me: I was born in St. Vincent's Hospital in Portland in the early 1950s and very soon thereafter adopted. My adoptive mother had been stricken with cancer (the verb is accurate – she was *stricken*). Her treatment had made it impossible for her to conceive children, so she and my father had sought to adopt. As a child, I must have had many questions that I voiced from time to time, but like all children, I learned to read my parents' moods and realised that this was both a deeply important and profoundly painful subject. Many years later, my wife asked my adoptive mother what she knew about my birth family, but there wasn't much to relate. In those days, the entire adoption process depended on secrecy.

In recent years, Oregon laws have made it possible for adoptees to obtain their original birth certificates, which I have done. No father is named there. A woman's name is hand printed in the box for "mother," but the cursive signature, by an entirely different hand, does not fully match the printed name. I can guess that a nurse filled out the form, but that my birth mother actually signed it. Her birthplace is an Oregon town I've never visited – one so small that I had to consult a map to determine its location.

Closed adoptions like mine rest on the living, daily embrace of fiction – an embrace that parents and children must learn to share. From the parents' view, one's children are not really one's children, yet they are. And the adopted child knows that one's parents are not really one's parents, yet they are. For me, this openness to fiction, to adoption as a larger idea, has lead to a sort of openness toward the world: anyone of the right age could function as mother or father figures, as siblings, as distant cousins. A long-running, thoroughly stale joke in our house claims my real parents were Marilyn and Elvis.

This embracing of fiction – the fiction of adoption – is similar to other beliefs affirmed in our daily lives. We believe in green pieces of paper in our wallets. As paper, it carries almost no intrinsic value, yet a twenty dollar bill gets me into a movie I want to see and yields some other paper and coins as well. Or it gives me something I'm happy to eat. We believe in property lines, even if we cannot always see them. We believe, sometimes now less fully, in our ability to make astonishing promises – like "until death do us part." Affirming such fictions brings an order we seek, and it creates value in the many understandings of that word.

Yet where others have what they would consider common-place knowledge, I have only absences, blanks. When a doctor asks me about my family's medical history, I can't offer any information. I can't look at photos of my mother's grandfather to gauge how much more hair I might lose or keep. I've never had the experience of seeing an aunt or uncle and finding in that face some resemblance to my own. Of course, I have photos from my adoptive family – and the stories to go with them. But, really, what is my relationship to those ancestors and their stories? How do I affirm this adopted history even as I know that there is another, truer one that has stayed utterly unsaid?

When people learn I'm adopted, they often ask if I want to know more about my birth parents and family. It's a question I wrestle with sometimes. Knowing nothing has its advantages, including the freedom to imagine whatever I wish. My mother discovered she was pregnant when she was seventeen. Second-to-last among five sisters, she has always known shared rooms and hand-me-down clothes. She has known about the mechanics of sex since she was little. But nothing prepares her for the experience of it – her body awake – his hands and lips, yes, but her body, hers. A small town resident, she keeps the secret of her pregnancy, though many of her friends and neighbours, eyeing her growing belly and thickening waist, guess at the truth. Her father, my grandfather, knows. But so long as nothing is said he pretends not to know. Her mother learns early and feels a disappointment she dare not acknowledge. Yet she also helps her daughter travel to family friends in Portland. Thus my mother lives with strangers until I am born. Then someone (that nurse who filled out my birth certificate) takes that infant away, thinking that under the circumstances this is a kindness, this is for the best.

"In the Blessed Absence of Television"

— John Burnside

If you knew where in the vacant lot
      past the prunings, leaves, bushes
hauled there to root or rot,
where weeds in their exuberance rose,
if you dug there, you found pink worms,
noodley segmented live things expanding
      and contracting, eager for the dark.
That place holds a house now — I don't know whose.
The creek goes in a concrete pipe,
but I remember it otherwise, as present
as outside and tonight.

If last spring we had children in this house,
      they would have seen the tenacity
of robins on a nest, an illustration
of whatever they would make of it: three eggs,
three robins fledged, all that slow construction
      and raucous hunger,
then, a second try and none to hatch.
They would have asked us to fix the injustice
      or explain the rules.

About the people who at my birth gave me up,
      I construct idle stories,
any of them in the making insufficient.
      I believe they are now both dead.
What is there to blame them for?
They greet me, the best of them,
in my daughters.
      As for secrets,
some we keep, and some keep us.

Tintern Abbey, Wales

Where ruins trouble time
    and common day, a halt wind
now whispers, now roars upriver
cold over the shoulders
    of hawthorns, hills unleafed,
all branches haze and confusion.

Here windows are windows yet
    unglassed, and roof is sky
where doves sail and calm
to choir, nave and aisle,
smooth tombs in a floor
    of grass.
The irreligious wondered here,
    or gazed.
The unconfessed trembled, and
prayers said or unsaid, chanted,
    sung, or cursed were once
numerous as hours.

Walls unroofed, east lights yet
open to sun. Lobed columns,
    a cloister, a warming room.
Quiet deepens and hallows day,
confirms around us and in us
answer and touch, laughter, hate,
    absence and presence together.

May the good dead love us
who know this place.

Night Sky Northwest

Ignorant of us, incapable of interest,
unacquainted even with water the simplest need,

all summer a dipper appears to revolve
slowly
        among uncountable lights,
though halogen bleaches them
and by carbons they are diffused.

Against the usual erasures, I look to them.
I'd like to know the names of my parents parents
parents parents – what they ate or wanted most to eat,
        and what, before sleep, they might have thought
but not discussed. Beyond their eyes, mouths, the
        circles of their faces, dirt under their nails,
I would like to know how they claimed for themselves
        importance and understanding – or
how they lived with not understanding.
It's not religion I mean, but what a mouth might say, how
        a face turns – the pauses, the
completions and the incompletions.

Of the dipper's handle and bowl, I presume some chart
        names each star.
They don't know what they don't know – when they
        began, how they writhe akin to each other, like suns.
Nor do they know their own light
steadily arriving
        where my eyes are drawn to look.

"My Father Is Telling Me the Story"

– W.S. Merwin

You have never known the pitch or timbre
of your father's voice nor the force
or shape of his hands nor the way his brow
furrowed as he squinted at small print
you have not known what he turned away from
closing the door except you are that person
you have not known what he made of night sky
or the way sun at dawn in November glistens
you have not known his shoes or watches or ties
his gait or religion or lack of it
nor his sisters nor his brothers
and of your mother you lack all the same
you look in the mirror and do not think of this now
you hear through the window a bird
you recognise but cannot name
you look in the mirror but not for who is there

3

"The Six Novels That Jane Austen Did Not Write"

— Virginia Woolf

You appear in the third, younger sister to
    a clergyman made unChristly rich
by the death of a dear elder cousin
who never married Mr. Eglid, her suitor, who
    died before her, of influenza, in March.
And you, sir, are the London barrister to whom
    a three day journey has fallen

to convey to Olivia, the sister,
that despite solicitor's advice, the terms of the
    will of her clergyman brother
make over to her *per annum*
the sum of 2000 pounds and the freedom of
    Alice House

built in 1763 for its namesake
by her father made gouty by Bombay cotton
    and Cotswold wool.
Dear Olivia, you need not marry
merely to roof yourself and your sweet soul.

Love whomever you love, including Miss Mary
    Augustana Farnsworth
who shall outlive you
and leave to your nephews and four nieces (our
    forbearers)
a thick portfolio – flowers, bridges, trees, creeks,
    a pencil sketch of a lawyer

all whiskers and a watch on a chain,
and these six of nine portraits she made of you
in watercolour, outside, in the same chair
    each August on your birthday.
They're on this table – we look at them now.

The Joy of Human Faces

They are pyracantha berries
    and the wrists and hips of roses.
They are the spring and ease of pine needles,
    the rigidities of spruce.
They are flat tin and corrugated tin, glass
    thinned to its certainties,
glass shaped to a palm for drink –
    simple water and bottled champagne.
They are chicory, gravel and oaks,
    the mucous of slugs,
sea palms, mollusks, the orange-footed birds.
    Pasture and stones.
They are sheilings, bog runnels and peat.
    Steeled wire and leaf mulch,
window screens, the flies inside and out.
    They are the breath of deer
bedded on a hillside in the sun.
    They are skunks' eyes,
otter fur, clouds arrived and gone,
    clouds on the way.
They are constellations and time,
    birth when they sing,
choir and the feathers of birds,
    iridescent, the blue
and the black. When they sing,
    it's song we breathe –
what we hear, what they are.

"I Noticed the Peaches"

– Christopher Howell

They're common anyone can
notice them except now and then they

ripen in the mind
the fuzz of their exterior become

a collusion of fingers and the feeling brain
the tongue retelling its own involvement

then wind sets loose an actual shimmer
of pastel and flutter it being April

and you realise you're seeing them
impersonal as they are

you hold a weight and liquid sweetness
not like memory

but a completion to believe in

Early Summer

On the wide verandah,
deep in a sloped-back cane chair dark in the shade,
I look out to a tree I saw once on the cover of a book
about a girl who grew up in Africa
and kissed each of the walls of her room when she left
as promise, a guarantee she would return.
We never do. If god walked up the steps,
and Walt Whitman with Cleopatra Queen of the Nile,
I would offer them iced tea with oranges.
We would look out, and just as now
I would wait to hear whatever I would hear.

★ ★ ★

Across the Arno, a mile from the Duomo,
on the hot, emptied stones of Florence,
I would like to lay on my back, look up at blue
then close my eyes, a pleasant heat under me.
I would know the name of the piazza and its church,
the one with Michelangelo's tomb decorated by Vasari —
poor Vasari, his best successes inevitably compared.
I would wake to day and time, say the Italian for olives,
the smaller and the larger, and garlic, the green grapes
round exactly, neither sour nor sweet but both,
the lamb and the wine — and I would name
the people with me, each one known, including Iago,
trusted by no one, Iago who has become a clown.

★ ★ ★

We visited this house for sale — this veranda,
this house. The broker told us *it is what it is*.
Which seemed almost the same as *it is what you see*.
Which means everything depends on looking,
which is hard, as David Hockney has said,
and most people don't do it, though we try.

At Castlerigg, Cumbria

Thirty-eight Neolithic stones
     circle what they always have –
you if you're inside them, grass
     at your feet, sky if you look up.
The song they sing hasn't varied
     with Thursday or next week,
Caesar or Christ, Muhammad (Peace Be
     Upon Him), Siddhartha, Shakespeare,
Sappho or Mickey Mouse. Keats
     walked here, called it in his journal
The Druid Temple. Coleridge knew it,
     Wordsworth, Dorothy, me or you
the same. What one should do here
     isn't clear. The planet warms.
Sheep bleat. You try to think of time –
     it goes the same as wind, grass, rock, sky.
Walking the circle, touching each stone,
     I want their certainty. I want to say
what they say, so I can hear it.

"Hammer and Sickle, 1928"

– Tina Modotti

Arc of steel and line of wood,
the sickle curves out of the frame, a blade
      so often honed its curve has deepened.
Rasped and filed with spit, it silvers.
      Northwest to southeast,
the hammer's handle flares the length of its taper.
      Gouged, nicked, oiled by palms
all the occasions of its use, the narrow grain
      has risen in thin lines.
And twin-headed, one angled away, the face
      we see shows blank, shows smooth,
whatever it has done and been made to do.
      Barn, fence-rail, lintel,
window-sill, door. Hops, maize, wheat,
      sugarcane, barley, hay. Sickle below,
hammer laid over on a white sheet,
      the light nearly noon. Before symbols
come tools, hands, the chores of hunger,
      family, shelter, tools of joy.
All things wait. All things wait to be read.

"Young Woman Standing at a Virginal"

– Vermeer, 1670

Golden mullions. Light from the left
    wakes a cape's lavish blue, a flounce
of cream linen sleeves.

Back-gathered hair in a red chignon,
ringlets shadowing her face, she's standing
    at the keys

playing artifice, the simplest of music
in her parlour with the blue velvet chair.

On the wall, Cupid stands with his one card.
Beside him, framed, a hill, cloud, sky.

Even the virginal's wide lid is painted trees.
Those views say home. The gaze as she
    looks at you is sentimental:

love and melody all this time.

Insomnia, BBC World Service

Because I could not sleep, I listened.
A woman's undulant voice spoke of her rape
three years past, a tactic of war,
the child of that afternoon asleep in her arms
until its crying interrupts the translator's English.
What happened to your husband?
They made him watch, then killed him.

Mark Twain said "the world owes you
nothing − it was here first."
But he had not heard this woman
singing to her waking boy.

"What Was There Before and Is There Still"

— Robert Creeley

This June week the Battle of the Somme
edges ever further from fear to history of fear.
Daughters and sons of the sons and daughters —
nephews, nieces, the grands and greats —
maybe they have pictures. Maybe they repeat
repeated stories in Gaelic, German, English, French.
Names in stone go meaningless.
Tomorrow at nine, local church bells will percuss.

Experience and the memory of it
inform my Gershwin's "Rhapsody in Blue."
Of course, I never met him, Gershwin.
I've seen David in Florence, Darwin
in a bronze chair in Shrewsbury, Lincoln in marble.
In Pontormo's frescos in San Felicita,
a young woman's face is promised a child,
and on another wall, her grief.

What was there before and is there still —
thirst and the crescent moon, Li Po.
Love of wine, love of touch.

A Greeting of Books

Importunate, mild, ineffable, unknown and clear,
Each at home, the most composed of guests —
Books lean at you. From their rooms of utterance,
They proclaim all manner of human invitation.

Keeping what the endlessly old world gives
To the endlessly arriving now, they would inquire:
They wish to know your questions —
The ones asleep and those awake.

They ask what you assume obvious, hence sure.
What in your breathing the day's air announces.
What and whom you would wish and claim and keep.
Read: their answers are their answers.

But yours are this week's, inchoate, unuttered — not yet.
A library's quiet is their answers waiting on yours.
And in their diffident, ever-curious chorus,
They encourage you: understand the dense and airy,

Consequential and not, dry and wet —
The water on your tongue. Understand the night
And all its stories. Listen, speak all,
And understand the day.

First Light

Now they crowd the horizon.
All night they have gathered there
confused, unable to converse,
stunned about timelessness
and what comes next.

I don't know them
but they anger me. Overnight,
they died of malaria, AIDS, tuberculosis,
dysentery, starvation, bullets, machetes,
while I slept in

in dreams happily now forgot,
body rested, coffee made, cloudy,
57 degrees, a light dew in calm winds.
Who was it said *the world is too much with us*?
Who was it said *we must risk delight*?

Clouds shift. Poplars leaf.
Starlings are a comfort:
nasty, merely birds,
they have shat their white
on three windows.

"To Live in Your Time"

— Adrienne Rich

To live in your time,
claim the windows you walked past and
   looked into all your childhood,
your parents, actual or not, sisters and
   brothers, the cousins you saw once a summer —
only start from there, what you say
about what cannot be said.

People in my time starve: they are starving now.
Because they are thirsty they drink water that will
   kill them or only their elderly, or only their
   children.
Yet studios and stray tables and concert halls make
   and museums keep safe extraordinary beauty.

People in my time wear the same watches.
At crosswalks they stand quietly but really they
   fear they cannot be distinguished one from another.
People in my time are comfortable
looking neither right nor left.
They embrace their own

or they have reached the end of their rope.
They like toys. They wonder, or they hate with such
   ferocity they kill themselves to become visible
   in dying
despite the privilege of breath

which they have forgotten
and the common confusion
and promise of touch.
People in my time do not trust the here or now —
it never stays long enough.

Pacific or Not

Pacific or not, the skies of my heart are coloured by
    the sea. Colour of doves, they bunch like fleece.
They call to their upper reaches muslin and linen.
They rain.
Blackened, they go, some mornings, all the hues to blue.

The landscape of my heart breathes trees, and under them
    mosses, creeks, trillium.
Basalt uplifts and snow make a year of advances
    and of retreats.
Thus the waters of the landscape of my heart
ice the hands that cup them, and for the love of trout
    feed caddis and mayflies,
and offer for maniacal salmon gravel, cascades and
    pools: leaves drift, wet pebbles shine.
Breeze through shade is balm.

The air of my heart is fog, is dew and clear, wood smoke,
    salt and wet. Its notes fill my ears.
It colours fire, blooms roses and apples,
and warms the slumped naps of summer afternoons.

Muddy roiling, a river arriving, a river going away,
bridges make the cities of my heart.
Walking over, we pause, some of us: we lean on our arms
    and look.

And as for the people of my heart, of only a few
    do I know their names
and they know who they are.

"The World Has Never Been Described Anywhere"
– Adam Zagajewski

Certainly not those half-black oaks
at the end of the gravel, past the five goats,
throats almost human with intercoursal joy.

Certainly not night crawlers after delugious rains,
nor Saturn before dawn. And what are 34 years
waking one person next to the other?

Viva la vida, says Frida Kahlo, and who'd say no?
I should read more, work and listen harder: time
is the class, earth the ripe impossible school.

Oak Fallen

It never knew itself as oak
or old or anything but root, trunk,
leaf, an ecology of collaboration.
Part dirt, part air and moon,
part dim and blinding sun,

it made of itself lifetimes
of shade and pattern, lichen, a habit of crows.
It made of itself a majesty
of instruction so intricate, commonplace
and intimate, we feel the loss.

Earth speaks the one language it knows.
Obligations and gratitudes, pleasures,
courage, joy – we make of it what we make.
One oak is a sand in the cosmos.
It is the fact and mystery we celebrate.

"We Must Trust Our Hope to Prevail"

– Robert Penn Warren

Hail will ever batter the roses.
A mother's chin echoes in one daughter;
for another, her father's curly hair.
You will go, though you don't want to.
Religions, friends, and countries go wrong.
Pick a tree-ripe orange for sugar in your palm.
The centipede brain seems never to stumble.
Spasms are what muscles know to teach.
You will go, though you don't want to.
Success unclear, work is the surer gift of work.
As I drove, you slept, and rain turned snow.
Next winter, next spring, no one has known.
I will go, though I don't want to.
We are changed seeing someone die.
One air, one ocean, one sky.

"One Day I Believe, Another I Disbelieve"
— *Czeslaw Milosz*

An acorn drops from the oak you walk
    under.
Another explodes behind you, as though
the tree itself resents mobility, the freedom
    of feet and of birds, resents what you
were thinking, hence not seeing the oak's own
    grandeur of location and persistence.

Then there is the rumoured truth – galaxies,
    for example, the milk
of the milky way at once visible and a blur.
Part of you knows what you see is light arriving
    from unknowable distances.
Endlessly old news. Or it's just milk.

Part of the confusion belongs to
how memory calls to mind the face
    and voice you have seen stilled,
even your own face and voice as a child
    in a world now photographs
of what is disappeared.

One looks at one's hand
and tries to understand how it came to be
    skin, tendon, nerve as it is,
and how volition's currents control it, callus
    and scar,
and how caress becomes violence,
and what punishment is just
and what forgiveness is.

"It's as Beckoning as Heaven"
– Richard Ford

We'd have our own lists –
the deodar cedars fog-frozen this morning:
white, heavy green near a mountain ash
    winter clear of leaves,

every contortion thorned with frost.
Seeing goes so unavailable some days it
    won't register regardless of what there is.
Anger does that, or grief, one of the intimations.

Or it might be achievement, ecstasy,
as in labour, as in a birth.
The sweetness of a good Satsuma tells me
    December, the pleasures of detachment.

Here's global warming, malaria for dinner,
    send money, spend more.
Or water in a glass.
Pink and white carnations.

Gravity, praise it, perseveres.
And the physics of planets and distance
brings breath and makes this – I mean this,
    this snow.

Beginning

Sky repeats its pallet of colours –
hereabouts especially triumphant grays.
Canes repeat their fruit, the blue and black
engorged sweetnesses of juice – Marion
or Tayberry or the red-to-almost-wine
raspberry sugar, colour of sun.

The branch repeats the trunk, then
the branch repeats the branch it came from.
The trunk repeats, I don't know how, the seed.
And I am my parents, but not, but not.

Your eyes repeat only your eyes.
They sleep sometimes and I watch them
sleeping and moving. They look at skies.
They read. Sometimes they read me.
Steam cooling repeats the water it was.
Yet the first child is unique
and the second child is unique
and what you will say to me and I to you
is not said until we begin.

"If Ending Is Air, Then Why Not Happiness?"

– Tim O'Brien

Starlings when they light on the roof sound
    like water.
Evening after a hot June day, noon higher
    than the record, then later, wind off the
planet's largest sea. The book ends.
It rests on the table, a planet, as Wallace
    Stevens said. Fans hum.
I think of places on the other side of the earth,
smells or sounds or touch I remember, faces
    and names,
the room down the hall, the one I slept in,
    or nights I rested on ground
by a creek noisy with snowmelt
and let it lull me
     after I stopped staring at stars.
June glide is slow delicious time.
Everything is choice and nothing is.
God is what or who knows the difference.

"Immediately After Christmas, the Mood Lightened in Manor Road"

– Andrew Motion

Aunt Lillian's hives subsided
and the dog's catarrh resolved with a packet of beef gristle
expelled as we listened to the symphony.
Blocked for a fortnight by snow, the glazier's van arrived at last
to replace the makeshift cashmere window plug
required after the crow flew through lead came and glass
and fell dead on an open page of the Oxford English Dictionary,
"C" volume, its black neck broken.

After multiple gin fizzes, Mother has arrayed herself in silks
and George's Stetson. She dances to Muddy Waters
with Father in his bear costume, complete with growling.
Uncle Winslow burnt the tree in a roar –
a wonder the chimney survived, and
the several second cousins have formed fruitcake
into balls they now roll for tenpins in the hall.

Outside, we're delighted how bells peal
and the human voice carries over snow. Walter calls.
Edna sends her best regards, as do Maude and Frank.
I wept a little this morning, thinking of poverty,
illness, the numberless orphans –
thank God no more talk of presents.

Winter sunlight, winter dark –
they are the best, don't you think? Must go
with all our love or this shall miss the post,
though I know there is always something more,
something important I have forgot.

Notes

"In My Alternate Life"
Untitled, 1949 is the name of a Mark Rothko painting.

"Foxglove, Bedstraw, Meadowsweet, Cow Parsley, Ragged Robin"
Gillian Clark in "Mass of the Birds," *Selected Poems*, p. 88.

"In Step and On Time"
Charles Wright in "Mount Caribou at Night," *The Southern Cross*,
and in "Scar Tissue II," *Scar Tissue*.

"Taking Any Route, Starting from Anywhere"
T. S. Eliot in "Little Gidding," *Four Quartets*.

"All Is a Procession"
Walt Whitman in "I Sing the Body Electric."

"We're Drowning in Explanations"
Shirley Hazzard, *New York Times* interview, Nov. 20, 2003.

"The Heart Wants What It Wants"
Emily Dickinson, as quoted in Alfred Habbegar's biography *My Wars
Are Laid Away in Books*, p. 445.

"To Own What Is Lost"
Lee Bassett in "The Fourth of July," *The Poems of Lee Bassett 1973-2000*,
p. 142.

"Their Smiles at the Camera Are of Genuine Delight"
Ian McEwan in Part One of *Black Dogs*, p. 3.

"I Wonder if Everything Has a Soul?"
Ellen Glasgow in *Barren Ground*, Grosset & Dunlap, 1925, p. 11.

"The Truth Is Never Loud"
Marjorie Sandor in "Elegy for Miss Beagle," *Portrait of My Mother
Who Posed Nude in Wartime*, p. 50.

"Time Lies All Around Us"
Peter Davison in "Finding Time to Write," *The Phi Beta Kappa Key
Recorder*, April 2001 (reprinted online at www.randomhouse.com).

"Nothing Happened That Night"
Kurt Vonnegut in *Slaughterhouse Five*, Delta paperback, p. 210.

"In the Blessed Absence of Television"
John Burnside in *A Lie About My Father*, Jonathan Cape, p. 287.

"My Father Is Telling Me the Story"
W.S. Merwin in "A Calling," from *The Pupil*, 2001, p. 31.

"The Six Novels That Jane Austen Did Not Write"
Virginia Woolf in her essay "Jane Austen."

"I Noticed the Peaches"
Christopher Howell in "Birdsong," *Oregon Literary Review*, Vol. 2, No. 1, Winter 2006.

"Hammer and Sickle, 1928"
Tia Modotti photograph.

"What Was There Before And Is There Still"
Robert Creeley in "To Think…" in *On Earth*, p. 5.

"To Live In Your Time"
Adrienne Rich, quoted by Heidi Benson in the *San Francisco Chronicle*, March 29, 2005.

"The World Has Never Been Described Anywhere"
Adam Zagajewski in *Another Beauty*, translated by Clare Cavanagh, p. 84.

"We Must Trust Our Hope to Prevail"
Robert Penn Warren in section III of "To a Little Girl, One Year Old, in a Ruined Fortress" in *Selected Poems 1923-1975*, p. 221.

"One Day I Believe, Another I Disbelieve"
Czeslaw Milosz in "Treatise on Theology," in *Second Space*, p. 62.

"It's as Beckoning as Heaven"
Richard Ford in *The Lay of the Land*, p. 194.

"If Ending Is Air, Then Why Not Happiness?"
Tim O'Brien in *The Lake of the Woods*, p. 299.

"Immediately After Christmas, the Mood Lightened in Manor Road"
Andrew Motion in *Philip Larkin, A Writer's Life*, p. 51.

About the Author

Born and raised in Portland, **Lex Runciman** has lived most of his life in Oregon's Willamette Valley. *Starting from Anywhere* is his fourth collection of poetry, following *Luck* (1981), *The Admirations* (1989) which won the Oregon Book Award, and *Out of Town* (2004). He holds graduate degrees from the writing programs at the University of Montana and the University of Utah. A co-editor of two anthologies, *Northwest Variety: Personal Essays by 14 Regional Authors* and *Where We Are: The Montana Poets Anthology*, his own work has appeared in several anthologies including, *From Here We Speak*, *Portland Lights* and *O Poetry, O Poesia*. He was adopted at birth. He and Deborah Jane Berry Runciman have been married thirty-seven years and are the parents of two grown daughters. He taught for eleven years at Oregon State University and is now Professor of English at Linfield College, where he received the Edith Green Award in teaching in 1997.

More Praise for *Starting from Anywhere*

These poems demonstrate that by starting from any-
where a poet can arrive somewhere. It doesn't mat-
ter if he starts with a wool cap or a Rembrandt. The
poet snatches at it, follows it, sees where it takes him
(wise passiveness) or where he can take it (supreme
fiction). Often a scrap from another writer prompts
him, or the rare visit to Tintern Abbey or Little Gidding.

Runciman never challenges his subject to a rule-bound
contest; he is never sure of entirely naming or
accounting for it. Only because "all things wait to be
read" and "the world has never been described any-
where," does he, as recipient and inventor, make
something of each encounter: "a completeness to
believe in," the location of "here," the finished poem.

Erik Muller